Gestation

poems by

Johanna DeBiase

Finishing Line Press
Georgetown, Kentucky

Gestation

Publisher: Leah Maines

Editor: Christen Kincaid

Cover Art: Johanna DeBiase

Author Photo: Judith Debiase, Judith Debiase Design

Cover Design: Elizabeth Maines McCleavy

Order online: www.finishinglinepress.com
              also available on amazon.com

Author inquiries and mail orders:
Finishing Line Press
P. O. Box 1626
Georgetown, Kentucky 40324
U. S. A.

Table of Contents

For my love, Eric, an amazing husband, father and human being.
And for Flora Galena, my heart walking around outside my body,
I am so proud of the young woman you have become.
Thank you both for being my home.

Winter

Early Symptoms

Perfect pregnancy is formulaic, prepared
months ahead; first a house, then a goat,
a garden, friends with children. All smoking
and drinking ceased. At least two more years
of young marriage. A feeling described as "ready."

The house felt cold that morning. I wore
thick socks and fleece sweaters. Sunlight
limited to low southern windows; the only
snow left hid in shadows. I considered
how many months before the light again.
Two lines, pink, innocent, appeared
immediately, to tell me unquestionably.

Quiet, my husband looked equally
in shock. My mother called, spontaneously
to share with me: it was Friday night in
New York and she just returned home with
a movie and Chinese food, like we used to do.
I told her the news. All was fine, she counseled.
In the 60's, no one knew any better.

Embryo

Poisoned with herbs, drowned in
alcohol, smothered in smoke, it
would not abort its mission; grew
without permission in the pliable
cavity hollowed out for its sowing
since my own growing began.

Packing resentment for
every nauseous moment,
each frailty cursed upon
my once indestructible
body, I carelessly crossed
continents to virus endemic
country sides, ate street food
with the look of spoiled
flesh, as if to say, oh yeah,
see if you can handle this.

Then I met with
the ocean, deep
tongue taking me
in rapid, rhythmic,
cellular beatings
both expelling and
cradling me to shore.

Breathing
life into me
twice the spirit
I used to be.

Volcano

I climbed a volcano today
to give you fire. Fearlessly
because the molten river crumbled
beside me, my rubber soles

immobile and melting over
hollow black rocks, my lungs burning
from the smoke pyre that billowed
out of the livid mountain core.

Over my shoulder, the sun set
in lava and plum hues and the
darkness turned the crust lip of peak
to shadow. Your father held my

hand as he guided me blind back
down the steep trail, night air
cooling the sweat from my body.
You, a flimsy pea, in abdomen

forming organs and spine, climbed
a volcano today. You will have
fire, to breathe, to spit, to
stand on, unflinching and bold.

Sometimes

Strength gives way to uncertainty, a faltering edge light
is meant to walk upon, no longer controlling but
now channeling a mass entity of tides and
probability where there is an open end
for all results to culminate through
and ceaseless worry to
either exasperate or
disintegrate.

Spring

Spring

More in bloom than
fruit blossoms and
willow buds, more
songs than robins
and magpies guarding
young nests, more
sweet scents than sage
on wind or earth
after rain. Invisible,
intangible, indistinct to
anyone but me, this
growing, when I laugh
and my belly reverberates
with extra life or
when I cry as if from
some other source, when
my neck aches to my
temples or my voice is
rasp with unintentional
contempt. When my surface
rounds and releases, my
own spring emerges
and I know now it is not
just sunshine and pretty
things but also storm clouds,
obscurity, and prey.

Ultrasound

You are curled up and potential
like a Firebelly Toad beneath
a root covered in moist morning
leaves, waiting to leap to life.

Made visible, you wave little
limbs as if a bright light disturbs
your new sleep. We are in well-lit
waiting rooms or sprawled on metal

tables with quirky British doctors
and fancy beeping machines to see
inside of us, to see you. We are
laughing and you are naïve to the

world, to joy or discontent while
you tuck away in fresh flesh and
grow without pause. Outside the
office door, sunlight warms my face.

About the Heartbeat

lost in pounding of
mama's belly pulse—
first echo of life,
thin vibrato, distant
giggles, tiny chimes,
bouncy balls between
two fused grins,
the wonder of a system
that keeps this sound
safe in unanimously
known and new-found
recesses of body doubling,
body unfurling and
taking what it needs,
filling up,
pumping fuel from
and bringing light to
secrets under skins—
speeding engine, fisted battery,
paper lantern.

First Mother's Day

They were everywhere,
dancing with clowns,
dueling with foam swords,
bopping each other
on the head with red,

green, yellow, balloons
all painted with smiley
faces. Sometimes, chasing
blue ones around the
grass, laughing, every one

of them, even after
falling or being told
it was time to go.
They ran between our
dancing skirts and we

took small steps not to
trample them. Blond curls
and black waves and red
knotty meshes like my
own hair at their age.

Scattered about in all
directions, I had to sit
to stop spinning. "Get
used to it," Sarah said
and I laughed, rubbing

my ripe belly. Yet, could
not imagine this new
world below my knees,
the tiny people and their
original awareness.

Summer

Our Meeting

There was a time, we were foreigners in
our own country where we had always thought

we would be at home or at least safe with
recognizable things like traffic leading

to stop lights, supermarkets, restaurants,
telephones without echoes. Alone, we

grasped at dark corners of a vast
white landscape hoping to pull back a page,

find an expression of something known. We
searched over shoulders and found strangers who

seemed to contain our longing in their
tight-lipped cages, to wring dry our dripping,

wet with afterbirth, in their long, loose
apertures, but instead we were suffocated

or disfigured or, worse, ignored. That was
where we found each other—

somewhere in the crowds of the great hall, the
potlatch ceremony, our stomachs growling

at steaming food that would soon be piled too high
on our plastic plates or perhaps it was

on the wire staircase ascending to
your studio where I first heard your voice

broadcasting messages to the phoneless
across rivers and mountain villages

or it might have been the autumn trail we
took too late at dusk to make camp in moonlight

and stay up staring at fire, drinking
cheap liquor. Not an instant embrace but

more a getting used to, a pushing to
see how far we could take it before all

folded back on itself, ourselves, where
we were soft cocoon among predators

and secret mates on a sinking ship. I
always left in summertime while you stayed

to brave mosquito swarms and fend off
drunken women. I liked to imagine

you circling the same five miles to the
dump and back, no longer searching but as

me, inviting, arriving, revealing.
There was no more darkness then,

safe in the knowing of each one's existence.

Summer Anniversary

A pomegranate torn open
at seam so the seeds seek outward
what they'd rather keep in to convey.
When day is late or earth's rotation

too slow, I hold you, cup the soft
skins that contain the juicy red
pulp, and, in turn, you hold me,
elegant thumbs like staples across

my gashed innards. Cradled, we leak with
dormant fears, still shy of breath
and dust. These shifting, mended grips, the
ordinary result of a mystical seal,

a marriage, that re-gifts
broken fruit to the vine,
each new season, whole again,
continues its growing.

The Nursery

We bashed in walls when we moved here, tore
up floors, destroyed remnants of past owners to
make it our own. The remaining *saltillo* tiles pave

a walkway through living space and kitchen to
back rooms polished with white paint soon to be
marked by short sticky fingers. A room of her own,

a corner, a niche, a chapter, absent of usual crib,
there are shelves for her clothes and portraits to
encourage tradition. The shade, seafoam like

a crayon but bright with white like lichen or
wet stones on a northern seashore. Already,
a soft pink chair for nursing quietly in the corner

where I can bathe her in sunbeams. With windows
ajar, the sounds of our river tumbling west through
the canyon hurriedly to town, errands to run perhaps,

and, at night, the coyotes whooping like a party of
drunken teenagers on the mesa top above us. This
home is for her more than ourselves. We could

live in shacks without water, in dirt piles along
highways but for baby we have rooms and room
to grow and green roofs and lucky blue doors.

Heart to Heart

In the soft blue hovering
haze of dawn you hold
my belly between your
hands and head, soft curls
and rough brush of unshaven
cheek, you whisper in a
voice that is between you
two only, soft and silly
and turning over rocks to
discover what lives beneath.
I laugh; baby learns your
voice with the trill of
my abdomen muscles—
tiny excited waves and
shuddering after quakes.
This morning, you tell baby,
I love you and what should
have been unsurprising
occurs to me: that you,
we, I might love this
unknown being still a part
of me, as if I would love
an organ that is simply
doing its job. It grows
only as I know my own
growth, breathes only as I
know my own breath, how
much my heart is full or
still has room for filling.

Belly Rolls

Middle is no longer my own—
still attached to me, allowing me
to connect limbs to limbs, yes, but
now inhabited by another. No longer

viable to bend in half, to pick up items
from the floor, put on shoes, pet my
dog, shave my legs, etcetera. There is
a bulbous skin-tight element and often,

the creature within takes turns shifting,
stretching, kicking or whatever nimble
movements can occur in such a cramped
space. The newspaper I lean onto my new

belly shelf jumps when the other motions
and sometimes, my favorite, a heel or
elbow stiffens against my rim like fingers
pushing out from within a latex glove or

jabbing Jell-O with the underside of a spoon,
and I can feel the little one within as if it were
reaching out to greet me, just for a moment
before the tumbling and acrobatics begin again.

False Alarm

Pain, a strong grip squeezing,
twists my torso taut; too active,
dehydrated, undernourished,
any of the above, my cervix

found too short for satisfaction.
Strapped inside the delivery room,
wide planks and skinny beds,
machines register crest and

trough delineations contracting
between dangerous and secure,
scrutinized by strangers in the next
room. Fifty minutes and missed

appointments, I leave, bloody
urine, but no activity: no walks, no
swims, no shopping, no painting, just
cry, the worry, the stress. My life a new

pace, deemed unfortunate, as if the
gentle rolls of body into place or the
cradle of belly in palms were not
enough, now stagnant, moribund,

beached. At rest so baby can grow to
breath on its own, breathing now—
deep breaths, all I can do, breath,
grow, and birth; breath, grow and birth.

Autumn

Nine Months

I am full as moon in
belly—shining and
round—awaiting
my waning.

These Last Few Days

Enveloped by the constancy of
mystery before you join us amongst
the oxygen: red blood, white cloud,
copper's hardy green skin. Each day
may be the one you voyage through
my body, thick and protruding. I topple.

My pelvis creaks; my throat on fire.
Will I shriek and cry pitched to keep
you in or will I groan and howl animal
to let you out? Will you be eager and
situated to pass through bone, muscle,
skin or will you raise an elbow, knee, brow,

to incubate just a while longer? The light,
though dim, the air, though moist, never the
perfect accommodations of your growing.
Regardless, I will deshell you from my
insides, peel open and dish out what I have
become for so long and peer into your eyes.

Birth, as It Was Made Known to Me

I. The First Twelve Hours

Amniotic fluids, just moments ago
supporting baby, fall in pools where
I stand. Broken membrane like a ticking
clock, a bomb nine months in the making,
twenty-four hours to countdown. We
lock the door behind us; we will
not return alone. Hot water, left running,
forms a rust ring around the white
sink in our four days absence.

II. The Second Twelve Hours

Flush out my insides; strip the excess.
On the far edge of town, midwives
mix their brew, herbs, tinctures, teas,
and oils, until the coming and going
of body squeezing and loosening takes
hold. In the tub, dunk in the prevailing
force, pain is a reluctant embrace.

III. The Next Twelve Hours

Ache ebbs from my body. Any
other time a good thing, this time
sinks like loss. We sleep from
dawn until the alarm. Time's up.

IV. The Last 10 Hours

Transport and belt to wires, tubes, needles,
pressure cuffs, machines, cords, monitors,
streams of paper, lines and graphs, hard
circle impressions on lasting belly bulge.
So begins my chemical induction.

Hours with strong hands on me, holding
me up, pushing me in, keeping me together.
Clenching muscles lift legs, twist tension
braids between bones. I let them paralyze me,
then lay back alone and quiet space. Relaxed,
I open like the yearning and crying of my hours.

V. The Last Half Hour

First there is fair hair, a soft skull,
my eyelids grip to expel, to turn inside
out. From canal to belly, we lift her
together, slippery flesh and white paste.
Wailing her welcome into our world, our
palms. Reverberating the delicate shell where
we meet her, new trio. Unaware even then,
cracked open and humbled.

Libra Baby

On the day of your birth, between
laborious breaths and the in and out
of consciousness, I glimpsed outside at dew
on gold leaves reflecting glass-like shimmers
                                        in the sun.

Born on autumn's cusp, when you inhaled
your first taste of fresh air, leaves rained
in the strong wind and frost gave way to snow.

Broke

When there is nothing left
her cries plunge me into debt,
her baby mammal wails
call down my electric milk
relieved into spread mouth,
open lips, tiny bird.

I have become
minutes passing
between her needs

where once I was
open road, fire building
and studious. New, sleepless
brain circulates, devoted
and dutiful in its search for
silent breath, heaving chest,
suckle and squeak,

always questioning her
presence and how
I will impede
on perfection.

J ohanna DeBiase is the author of the fabulist novella *MAMA & THE HUNGRY HOLE* (Wordcraft of Oregon, 2015), which was short-listed for the 2014 Serena McDonald Kennedy Award and referred to by Publisher's Weekly as an "exquisitely crafted debut novella."

She writes from New Mexico where she is spellbound by the energy vortex of Taos Mountain. Originally from New York, she earned her BA in Literature and Creative Writing from Bard College and her MFA in Creative Writing from Goddard College.

Her short fiction, flash and video poems have appeared in *Hayden's Ferry Review, Portland Review, Atticus Review, Monkeybicycle, Convergence, Prick of the Spindle and Queen Mob's Tea House,* among others.

She has received scholarships to attend Pikes Peak Writers Conference, Vermont Studio Center and San Miguel Writers Conference. She is a book reviewer, writing teacher, collage artist, yoga instructor and mother of one. Find her online at *www.JohannaDeBiase.com*

CPSIA information can be obtained
at www.ICGtesting.com
Printed in the USA
JSHW022047031120
9292JS00001B/26